CONTENT 2A

Hi, I'm Jack

Mini Talk Look and listen. ▶ 🎧03

> Hi, I'm Jack.
> What's your name?

> Hello.
> My name is Roboter.

> Bye, Roboter.

🎧04 CHECK 1 a ☐ b ☐ 2 a ☐ b ☐

Practice

A Listen and write the letter. 🎧05   **B** Listen and repeat. 🎧06

I'm Jane. What's your name?   My name is Min.

Jane ☐   Min ☐   Lily ☐   Ann ☐

Sam ☐   Rita ☐   Mia ☐   Kevin ☐

Listen & Talk

A Listen and stick. 🎧07

Write & Talk

A Listen, write, and read. 🎧 08

Hi	name
I'm	Goodbye

Hello, _____ Ben.

What's your name?

_____. My _____ is Kate.

_____, Tom.

Bye, Tina.

B Read and match. Then say.

1 Hi. I'm Tinker Bell.

2 Hello. My name is Peter Pan.

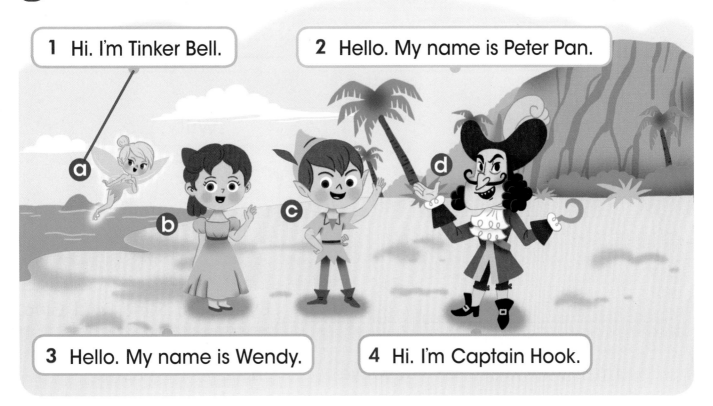

3 Hello. My name is Wendy.

4 Hi. I'm Captain Hook.

Story

Ⓐ Listen, write, and read. ▶ 🎧09

1

_____, I'm Willy.

Hi.

2

What's your name?

_____ Lina.

3

Hey, Lina!

_____ name is Mina.

4

Hey, Mina!

My _____ is Gina.

5

Mina! Gina!

....

6

_____, Willy.

Bye, Lina, Mina, and Gina.

| I'm | My | Goodbye | Hello | name |

B Read and match.

1

2

3

4

a My name is Willy.

c I'm Gina.

b I'm Mina.

d My name is Lina.

Challenge

Draw your face and write.

Hello.

My name is _____.

Ⓐ Listen and circle ○ or ✕. 🎧11

1

○   ✕

2

○   ✕

3
○   ✕

Ⓑ Listen and match. 🎧12

1

2

3

4

Lily

Tina

Kevin

Tom

Ⓒ Listen and choose. 🎧13

1

ⓐ   ⓑ

2

ⓐ   ⓑ

3

ⓐ   ⓑ

D Read, check, and write.

1

A: Bye, Willy.

B: _____, Emily.

☐ Hi ☐ Goodbye

2

A: Hello. _____

☐ I'm Alex. ☐ Bye, Jane.

B: Hi. My name is Jane.

3

A: What's your name?

B: _____

☐ Hello, Sam. ☐ My name is Ann.

E Write and say.

1

Jack

Hello, I'm Jack.

Mia

2

My name is Ann.

What's This?

Mini Talk Look and listen. 16

What's this?

It's a pencil.

What's that?

It's an eraser.

Oh, no!

17 CHECK 1 a □ b □ 2 a □ b □

Practice

A Listen and write the letter. 18

B Listen and repeat. 19

Listen & Talk

A Listen and circle. 🎧20

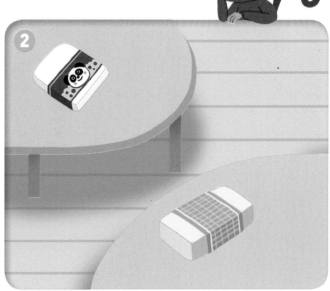

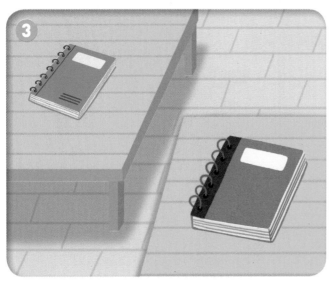

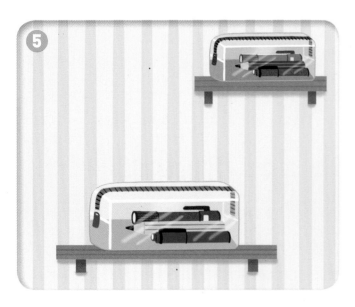

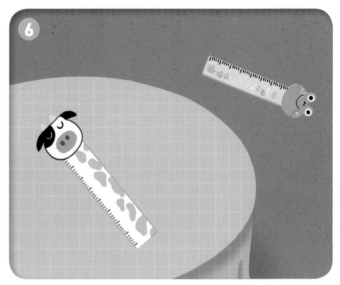

Write & Talk

A Listen, write, and read. 🎧 21

that	eraser
this	pencil case

😃 What's _____, Tina?

😊 It's an _____.

😃 Wow! It's good.

😮 What's _____?

😊 It's a _____.

😮 Oh, it's nice.

B Find and write. Then say.

This That

1 _____ is a ruler.

2 _____ is a notebook.

3 _____ is a pencil.

4 _____ is an eraser.

Story

A Listen, write, and read.

ball   that   book   this   pencil

14

B **Read and choose.**

1

      ⓐ It's a book.   ⓑ It's an eraser.

2

      ⓐ It's a ruler.   ⓑ It's a ball.

3

      ⓐ It's a pencil.   ⓑ It's a pencil case.

Challenge

Choose, draw, and write.

What's this?

_____

Song 23

A Listen and number. 🎧 24

B Listen and circle T or F. 🎧 25

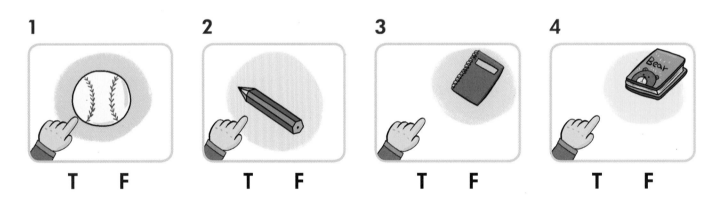

1 T   F

2 T   F

3 T   F

4 T   F

C Listen and choose. 🎧 26

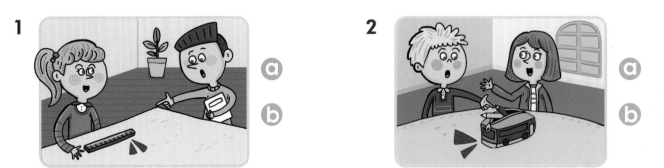

1 a   b

2 a   b

D Circle and write.

1

_____ is a pencil.
(This / That)

2

A: What's _____? (this / that)

B: It's _____. (a bag / a ball)

3

A: What's _____? (this / that)

B: It's _____. (a ruler / an eraser)

E Write and say.

1

What's this?

2

It's a ball.

Review 1

A Circle and write.

1 ((hi) / bye)   hi

2 (book / ball)

3 (bag / ruler)

4 (pencil / notebook)

5 (pencil / ball)

6 (pencil case / book)

7 (eraser / ruler)

8 (goodbye / hello)

B **Number and match.**

Hi. I'm Kate. •	• Goodbye, Ben.
Bye, Kelly. •	• Hi. My name is Lily.
What's your name? •	• My name is Bill.

C **Circle and write.**

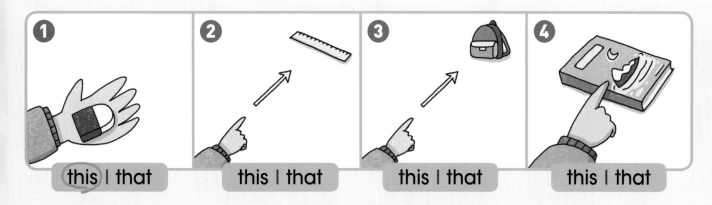

1 this | that
2 this | that
3 this | that
4 this | that

1 A: What's _____?
   B: It's an _____.

2 A: What's _____?
   B: It's a _____.

3 A: What's _____?
   B: It's a _____.

4 A: What's _____?
   B: It's a _____.

ruler
eraser
book
bag

Is That a Hen?

Mini Talk Look and listen.

Practice

A Listen and write the letter. 🎧31   **B** Listen and repeat. 🎧32

Is this a cow?

Yes, it is.

No, it isn't. It's a pig.

Yes

1 cow

2 hen

3 horse

4 rabbit

5 pig

No

6 cat

7 dog

8 duck

Listen & Talk

A Listen and circle ○ or X. 🎧 33

Write & Talk

A Listen, write, and read. 🎧 34

Look. Is _____ a cat?

_____, it is.

Wow! I like it.

What's this?

Is _____ a horse?

No, it _____. It's a _____.

B Connect and write. Then ask and answer.

pig   duck
rabbit   hen

1 Is this a _____?

Yes, it is.

2 Is this a cow?

_____, it isn't. It's a _____.

Story

Ⓐ Listen, write, and read. ▶ 🎧35

| cat | horse | dog | Yes | No |

B Read, check, and write.

1

Is this a cat?

☐ Yes, it is.
☐ No, it isn't. It's a _____.

2

Is this a horse?

☐ Yes, it is.
☐ No, it isn't. It's a _____.

3

Is this a pig?

☐ Yes, it is.
☐ No, it isn't. It's a _____.

Challenge

Choose one and write.

Is that a cow?

_____, _____ _____.

It's a _____.

Song

Check-Up

A Listen and choose. 🎧37

1

2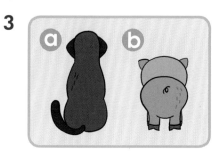

3

B Listen and circle ◯ or ✕. 🎧38

1 ◯ ✕

2 ◯ ✕

3 ◯ ✕

4 ◯ ✕

C Listen and choose. 🎧39

1

    ⓐ Yes, it is.

    ⓑ No, it isn't.

2

    ⓐ Yes, it is.

    ⓑ No, it isn't.

3

    ⓐ Yes, it is.

    ⓑ No, it isn't.

D Read, check, and write.

1

A: Is this _____?

☐ a duck ☐ a cat

B: Yes, it is.

2

A: Is that a dog?

B: _____ It's a horse.

☐ Yes, it is. ☐ No, it isn't.

3

A: Look. Is _____ a rabbit?

☐ this ☐ that

B: Yes, it is.

E Write and say.

1

Is this a cow?

2

Yes, it is.

This Is My Brother, Ken

Mini Talk Look and listen.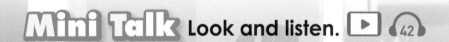

This is my brother, Ken.

Hello. I'm Tina.
Nice to meet you.

Nice to meet you, too.

That is my cat, Max.

Hi, Max!

CHECK 1 a ☐ b ☐ 2 a ☐ b ☐

28

Practice

A Listen and write the letter. 🎧44

B Listen and repeat. 🎧45

This is my grandfather.
Nice to meet you.
Nice to meet you, too.

father

grandfather

grandmother

father

brother

mother

sister

my dog

Listen & Talk

A Listen and stick. 🎧46

This is my family.

1 Amy

2 Kate

3 Ben

4 Tom

5 Tina

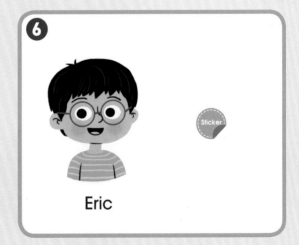

6 Eric

Write & Talk

A Listen, write, and read. 🎧47

father too name
Hello this

This is my _____.

Father, _____ is my friend, Eric.

Nice to meet you, Eric.

Nice to meet you, too.

_____, I'm Eva.

Hi. My _____ is Nick.

Nice to meet you.

Nice to meet you, _____.

B Look and write. Then say.

father mother
brother sister

1 This is my _____.

2 This is _____ _____.

3 _____ is my _____.

4 _____ _____ my dog.

Story

Ⓐ **Listen, write, and read.** ▶ 🎧 48

cat   Nice to meet you.   Hello   this   too   father

B Read and match.

1

2

3

a This is my friend, Pam.

b This is Fred.

c Nice to meet you.

Challenge

Check and write.

Lisa

Hello, I'm _____.

Nice to meet you.

This is _____ _____.

Song 49

Check-Up

A Listen and number. 🎧50

B Listen and mark ○ or ✕. 🎧51

1

2

3

4

C Listen and choose. 🎧52

1

a
b

2

a
b

This is my sister.　　This is my father.
Nice to meet you.

D Look and write.

1

A: _____

B: Hello, I'm Nick. Nice to meet you.

C: Nice to meet you, too.

2

Alex　　Jack

A: Hello, I'm Alex. _____

B: Nice to meet you, too. I'm Jack.

3

Eva　　Amy

A: _____

B: Nice to meet you. I'm Amy.

C: I'm Eva. Nice to meet you, too.

E Write and say.

1

Nice to meet you, too.

2

Nice to meet you.

Review 2

Ⓐ Look and write.

pig	duck	grandfather	grandmother
sister	horse	brother	cow	mother

B Read and mark ○ or ✗.

1 Is that a duck?
   No, it isn't. It's a dog. ☐

2 Is this a hen?
   Yes, it is. ☐

3 Is that a pig?
   No, it isn't. It's a cat. ☐

4 Is that a horse?
   Yes, it is. ☐

C Read and write in the order.

_____

_____

_____

ⓐ Nice to meet you, too.

ⓑ Father, this is Eric.

ⓒ Nice to meet you.

I Like Bread

Mini Talk Look and listen. ▶ 🎧55

I like bread.
How about you?

I like bread, too.

Is this a pig?
Yummy!

Yes, it is.

🎧56 CHECK 1 a ☐ b ☐ 2 a ☐ b ☐

Practice

A Listen and write the letter. 57   **B** Listen and repeat. 58

1 bread ☐

2 soup ☐

3 salad ☐

4 pizza ☐

5 fish ☐

6 chicken ☐

7 milk ☐

8 popcorn ☐

I like bread.
How about you?

I like bread, too.

Listen & Talk

A Listen and stick. 🎧59

1

2

3

4

5

6

Write & Talk

A Listen, write, and read. 🎧 60

I like _____. How about you?

I _____ cake.

I like cake, _____.

What's _____?

It's _____.

Oh, I _____ popcorn.

Thank you, Dad.

B Look and write. Then ask and answer.

I like pizza.
How about you?

chicken   milk
pizza   salad

1 I like _____.

2 I _____ _____.

3 _____ _____ _____.

4 _____ _____ _____.

Story

A Listen, write, and read. 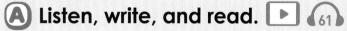 61

| like | bread | Milk | popcorn | pizza | fish |

B Look and circle.

1

I like (pizza / popcorn).

2

I like (bread / salad) and (milk / fish).

3

I like (pizza / soup).

 Challenge

Choose three things and draw. Then write.

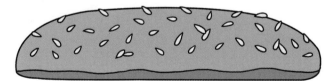 ☐ chicken ☐ salad ☐ fish ☐ pizza ☐ popcorn

I like _____ and _____.

I like _____, too.

 62 Song

Check-Up

A Listen and number. 🎧63

B Listen and circle ○ or ✕. 🎧64

1

○
✕

2

○
✕

3

○
✕

4

○
✕

C Listen and choose. 🎧65

1

ⓐ
ⓑ

2

ⓐ
ⓑ

D Look and write.

1

A: I like fish.

B: I like fish, _____.

2

A: I like cake. How about you?

B: I like _____.

3

A: Is this _____?

B: Yes, it is.

A: Oh, I like soup.

E Write and say.

1

I like popcorn.

2

I like chicken. How about you?

How Many Apples?

Mini Talk Look and listen.

How many apples?

Five apples.

No. Four apples and one ball.

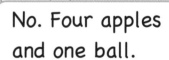

CHECK 1 a ☐ b ☐ 2 a ☐ b ☐

Practice

A Listen and write the letter. 🎧 70   **B** Listen and repeat. 🎧 71

How many watermelons? | Two watermelons.

Fruit House

1 two — watermelons ☐

2 three — apples ☐

3 four — bananas ☐

4 five — pears ☐

5 six — oranges ☐

6 seven — lemons ☐

7 eight — kiwis ☐

Listen & Talk

①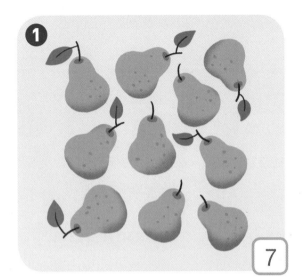
7

②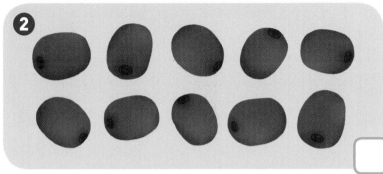

③

④

⑤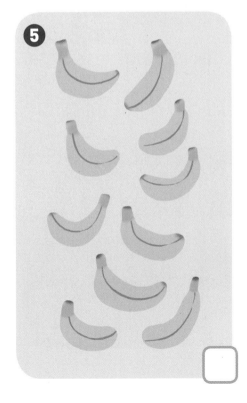

⑥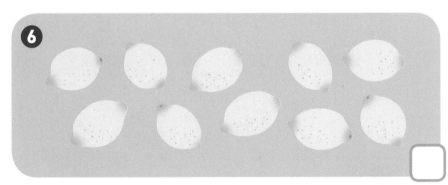

48

Write & Talk

Ⓐ Listen, write, and read. 🎧 73

Three	Ten	Five
bananas	many	like

🐵 I _____ bananas.

🐵 How many _____?

🐵 _____ bananas.

🐵 How _____ oranges?

🐵 _____ oranges. How about you?

🐵 _____ oranges.

Ⓑ Count and write. Then ask and answer.

How many ...?

1 _____ watermelons.

2 Four _____.

3 Six _____.

4 _____ kiwis.

5 Two _____.

Nine	Two	pears
lemons	apples	

Story

Ⓐ Listen, write, and read. ▶ 🎧 74

1 One watermelon, milk, and fish.

2 _____ pears.
How many _____?

Three _____ and six apples.

3 How many _____?
_____ bananas.

4

5 Five _____ and two lemons.

6 Dad, I like candy.
I like candy, too.

| Four | Seven | kiwis | bananas | oranges | pears |

B Look and match.

How many ...?

1

Four

apples.

2

Seven

bananas.

3

Six

pears.

Challenge

Choose one, draw, and write.

A: How many _____?

B: _____ _____.

Song 75

Unit 6 **51**

Check-Up

A Listen and choose. 🎧76

1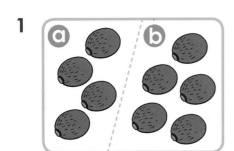

2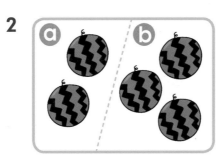

3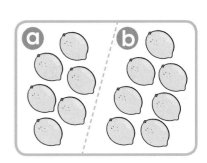

B Listen and circle ○ or ✗. 🎧77

1

○   ✗

2

○   ✗

3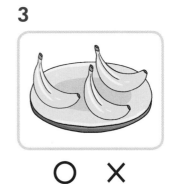

○   ✗

4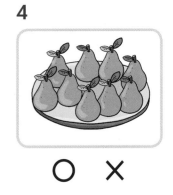

○   ✗

C Listen and match. 🎧78

1  ・

・ six ・

・ bananas

2  ・

・ nine ・

・ oranges

3  ・

・ ten ・

・ apples

D Read, circle, and write.

1

A: How many _____?

B: Five _____.
(lemons / watermelons)

2

A: How many kiwis?

B: Four _____.
(kiwis / bananas)

3

A: How many _____?

B: _____ pears.
(Seven / Eight)

E Write and say.

1

Five apples.

2

How many bananas?

Ⓐ Match and write.

1 p___p___orn

2 ___oup

3 s___la___

4 m___l___

5 pi_____a

6 p___a___s

7 ba___a___as

8 ___i___is

9 wa___er___elo___s

B **Read and write.**

How about you?   How many kiwis?   I like bread, too.

Seven kiwis.   Five oranges.

What Color Is It?

Mini Talk Look and listen. ▶ 🎧81

It's red.

It's yellow.
What color is it?

It's orange.

I like orange.

Practice

A Listen and write the letter. 83   **B** Listen and repeat. 84

What color is it?   It's pink.

1
2
pink ☐   orange ☐

3
green ☐

4
5
white ☐

black ☐

6
purple ☐

7
8
gray ☐

brown ☐

Listen & Talk

Listen and choose. 85

Write & Talk

A Listen, write, and read. 🎧86

What _____ is it?

It's _____. I like orange.

How about you?

I like _____.

What's that?

_____ a bag.

What color is it?

It's _____ and black.

B Look and write. Then ask and answer.

What color is it?

white

yellow

black

red

blue

purple

1   It's _____.   2   It's _____ and _____.

3   It's _____.   4   It's _____ and _____.

Story

A Listen, write, and read.

1. Blue?

2. I like _____.

3. It's _____.
   Thank you. I like orange.

4. It's _____.
   Thank you. I like black.

5. Oops! I'm sorry.
   That's okay. I like _____.

6. _____ is it?
   It's green.

7. Oh! It's yellow.

| What color | black | purple | brown | orange |

B Read and match.

1

What color is it?
It's orange.

•

•

2

What color is it?
It's yellow.

•

•

3

What color is it?
It's black and white.

•

•

Color and write.

It's a fish. What color is it?

It's _____.

I like _____.

88
Song

Check-Up

A Listen and choose. 🎧89

1
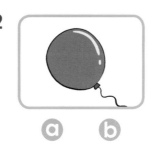
ⓐ   ⓑ

2
ⓐ   ⓑ

3
ⓐ   ⓑ

4

ⓐ   ⓑ

B Listen and match. 🎧90

1

2

3

4

C Listen and choose. 🎧91

1
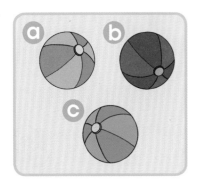
ⓐ   ⓑ   ⓒ

2
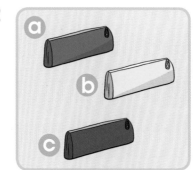
ⓐ   ⓑ   ⓒ

3
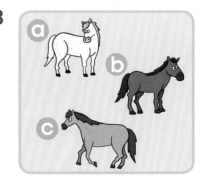
ⓐ   ⓑ   ⓒ

D **Read and write.**

> It's orange.   What color is it?
>   I like pink.

1

A: What color is it?

B: _____

2

A: It's a dog.

B: _____

A: It's brown.

3

A: Look! It's a rabbit.

B: It's pink. _____

E **Write and say.**

1

It's green. I like green.

2 What color is it?

Mini Talk Look and listen. ▶ 🎧94

Close the door, please.

Okay.

Wow!

Come here.

Okay.

Oh, no!

95
CHECK 1 a ☐ b ☐ 2 a ☐ b ☐

Practice

Sit down, please.   Okay.

1

2 come here ☐

3

open the window ☐

sit down ☐

6 stand up ☐

4

5

catch the ball ☐

close the door ☐

Listen & Talk

(A) Listen and match. 🎧 98

1

2

3

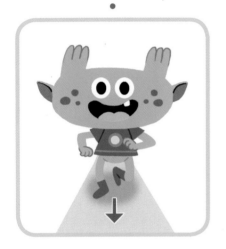

4

5

6

Write & Talk

A Listen, write, and read. 🎧 99

I'm	Thank you
Sit down	Open robot

Hello. What's your name?

Hello. _____ Kate.

_____, please.

Okay.

_____ the box, Ray.

Wow! It's a _____.

_____, Mom.

B Look and write. Then say.

Close	Open
Stand	Come

1 _____ here, please.

2 _____ up, please.

3 _____ the window, please.

4 _____ the door, please.

Story

A Listen, write, and read.

blue   Catch   Come here   Sit down   please

B **Read and match.**

1

2

3

Come • • down, please.

Catch • • here, please.

Sit • • the ball, Jack!

Challenge

Look and write. Then say.

1 _____, please.　　2 _____, please.

Check-Up

A Listen and choose. 🎧102

1
ⓐ ⓑ

2
ⓐ ⓑ

3
ⓐ ⓑ

4
ⓐ ⓑ

B Listen and number. 🎧103

○ ○ ○ ○

C Listen and mark ○ or ✕. 🎧104

1

2

D Look and write.

1

A: _____, please.

B: Okay.

A: Thank you, Kate.

2

A: _____, Tony!

B: Okay.

A: Good.

3

A: _____, please.

B: Okay. I'm sorry.

E Write and say.

1

_____, Anna.

Okay.

2

_____, please.

Okay.

Review 4

A Unscramble and number.

1 `r p u l e p` ⋯▸ __purple__

2 `n g e o r a` ⋯▸ _____

3 `r g n e e` ⋯▸ _____

4 `r a y g` ⋯▸ _____

B Circle and write.

1 _____ the door
(open / close)

2 sit _____
(up / down)

3 _____ the window
(open / close)

4 _____ the ball
(catch / close)

C **Read and write the letter.**

1 A: Stand up, please.
   B: Okay.

2 A: What color is it?
   B: It's pink.

3 A: Open the door, please.
   B: Okay.

4 A: What color is it?
   B: It's black.

5 A: Come here, please.
   B: Okay.

6 A: What color is it?
   B: It's brown.

Songs

Unit 1 Hello, I'm Jack 🎧 10

Hello, I'm Jack. What's your name?

Hello, Jack! I'm Kate.

Hi, I'm Rita. What's your name?

Hi, Rita! My name is Andy.

Goodbye, Jack!

Bye, Kate!

Goodbye, Rita!

Bye, Andy!

Unit 2 What's This? 🎧 23

What's this? What's this?

It's a ruler.

What's that? What's that?

It's a book.

What's this? What's this?

It's a pencil.

What's that? What's that?

It's a pencil case.

Unit 3 Is This a Hen? 🎧 36

Is this a hen?

No, it isn't. It's a duck.

Is that a dog?

Yes, it is. It's a dog.

Is this a cat?

Yes, it is. It's a cat.

Unit 4 Nice to Meet You 🎧 49

This is my brother, Kevin.

Hi, Kevin. Nice to meet you.

Nice to meet you, too.

This is my sister, Mei.

Hello, Mei. Nice to meet you.

Nice to meet you, too.

Unit 5 I Like Bread 🎧62

I like bread. How about you?

I like bread, too.

I like chicken. How about you?

I like chicken, too.

I like pizza. How about you?

I like pizza, too. Yeah!

Unit 6 How Many Bananas? 🎧75

How many bananas?

Three bananas.

How many kiwis?

Five kiwis.

How many oranges?

One, two, three,

four, five, six,

seven, eight!

Eight oranges!

Unit 7 What Color Is It? 🎧88

What color, what color is it?

Green! It's green.

Brown! It's brown.

What color, what color is it?

Purple! It's purple.

Pink! It's pink.

I like pink.

Unit 8 Come Here, Please 🎧101

Hey, Robo!

Come here, please.

Okay.

Sit down, please.

Okay.

Close the window, please.

Okay.

Good!

Ⓐ Listen, circle, and match. 🎧105

1		2		3		4	
b	p	s	z	r	l	f	v

Ⓑ Listen and write. 🎧106

s h m d b w

1	2	3	4

Ⓒ Look and write.

y l n v c g

1	2	3	4

___ est	___ ine	___ ion	___ at

Phonics ②

Ⓐ Listen and repeat. Then read. 🎧107

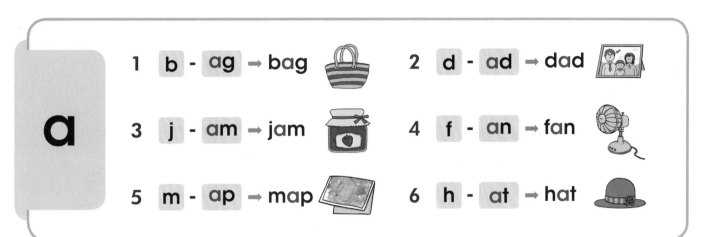

a

1 b - ag → bag

2 d - ad → dad

3 j - am → jam

4 f - an → fan

5 m - ap → map

6 h - at → hat

Ⓑ Listen and circle. 🎧108

1 bad   bag   bat

2 hat   ham   map

3 dad   van   bag

4 fan   map   mat

Ⓒ Read and match.

1 fan

2 dad

3 jam

A Listen and repeat. Then read. 109

 i

1 b - ig → big

2 p - in → pin

3 s - ix → six

4 m - ix → mix

5 s - it → sit

6 h - it → hit

B Listen and match. 110

1 p •   • ig

b •   • in

2 p •   • ix

m •   • in

3 s •   • it

h •   • ix

4 p •   • ig

s •   • it

C Unscramble and write.

1

t s i

[   ]

2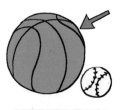

g b i

[   ]

3

i s x

[   ]

Phonics ④

Ⓐ Listen and repeat. Then read. 🎧111

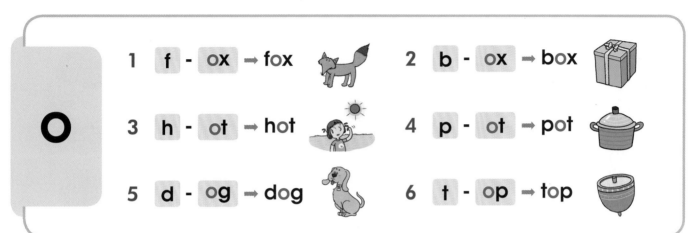

o

1 f - ox → fox

2 b - ox → box

3 h - ot → hot

4 p - ot → pot

5 d - og → dog

6 t - op → top

Ⓑ Listen and circle. 🎧112

1 hot   box   dog

2 pot   box   dog

3 fox   top   hot

4 fox   pot   top

Ⓒ Circle and write.

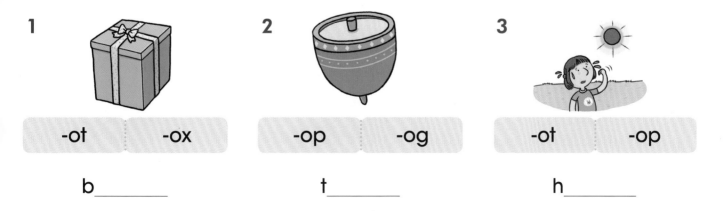

1 -ot   -ox

b_____

2 -op   -og

t_____

3 -ot   -op

h_____

A Listen and repeat. Then read. 113

u

1 n - ut → nut

2 c - ut → cut

3 c - up → cup

4 t - ub → tub

5 r - un → run

6 s - un → sun

B Listen and match. 114

1 t •   • ub
  r •   • un

2 s •   • ut
  n •   • un

3 c •   • ut
  n •   • up

4 t •   • ut
  c •   • ub

C Unscramble and write.

1

n s u

2

c p u

3

u t c

Phonics ⑥

Ⓐ Listen and repeat. Then read. 🎧115

e

1 b - ed → bed

2 l - eg → leg

3 h - en → hen

4 t - en → ten

5 j - et → jet

6 w - et → wet

Ⓑ Listen and circle. 🎧116

1	2	3	4
wet	leg	jet	leg
hen	jet	pen	red
bed	ten	bed	jet

Ⓒ Match and write.

1  •   t • • ed → [ ]

2   •   b • • en → [ ]

3  •  w • • et → [ ]

Phonics ❼

Ⓐ Listen, circle, and write. 🎧117

1 -ot -it ═══ h_____

2 -un -en ═══ t_____

3 -ix -ot ═══ s_____

4 -ig -ag ═══ b_____

Ⓑ Listen, circle, and match. 🎧118

1
run
fan
•

2
cut
jet
•

3
wet
sit
•

4
fan
pin
•

•

•

•

•

Ⓒ Circle and write.

1

-ag -ox

b_____

2

-og -ad

d_____

3

-ut -ot

c_____

Phonics ⑧

Ⓐ Listen and repeat. Then read. 🎧119

-ck
-ng

1 ck ➡ duck

2 ck ➡ kick

3 ck ➡ sick

4 ng ➡ ring

5 ng ➡ king

6 ng ➡ wing

Ⓑ Listen and check. 🎧120

1 ☐ -ck   ☐ -ng

2 ☐ -ck   ☐ -ng

3 ☐ -ck   ☐ -ng

4 ☐ -ck   ☐ -ng

Ⓒ Match and write.

1
du •   • ng
ki •   • ck

2
ki •   • ck
ri •   • ng

3
wi •   • ck
ki •   • ng

4
ri •   • ck
si •   • ng

Word List 2A

Unit 1 — Hi, I'm Jack

bye _____

goodbye _____

hello _____

hi _____

my _____

name _____

what _____

your _____

Unit 2 — What's This?

bag _____

ball _____

book _____

eraser _____

nice _____

notebook _____

pencil _____

pencil case _____

ruler _____

that _____

this _____

Unit 3 — Is That a Hen?

cat _____

cow _____

dog _____

duck _____

hen _____

horse _____

pig _____

rabbit _____

that _____

this _____

Unit 4 — This Is My Brother, Ken

brother _____

grandfather _____

grandmother _____

family _____

father _____

friend _____

mother _____

my _____

sister _____

Unit 5 — I Like Bread

and	_____
bread	_____
cake	_____
chicken	_____
fish	_____
like	_____
milk	_____
pizza	_____
popcorn	_____
salad	_____
soup	_____
too	_____

Unit 6 — How Many Apples?

apples	_____
bananas	_____
kiwis	_____
lemons	_____
oranges	_____
pears	_____
watermelons	_____

two	_____	six	_____
ten	_____	three	_____
nine	_____	eight	_____
seven	_____	five	_____
one	_____	four	_____

Unit 7 — What Color Is It?

black	_____
blue	_____
brown	_____
gray	_____
green	_____
orange	_____
pink	_____
purple	_____
red	_____
white	_____
yellow	_____

Unit 8 — Close the Door, Please

catch the ball	_____
close the door	_____
close the window	_____
come here	_____
open the box	_____
open the door	_____
open the window	_____
sit down	_____
stand up	_____

Syllabus 2A

Unit 1   Hi, I'm Jack

Structures	Vocabulary		Phonics
• Hi, I'm Jack.	hi	what	Review: Single Letters
• I'm Jane. What's your name?	hello	name	
My name is Min.	bye	my	
• Bye. / Goodbye, Rita.	goodbye	your	

Unit 2   What's This?

Structures	Vocabulary		Phonics
• What's this? It's a pencil.	bag	pencil	Short Vowel a
• What's that? It's an eraser.	ball	ruler	
• This is a ruler. / That is an eraser.	book	eraser	
• It's nice / great.	pencil case	notebook	

Review 1

Unit 3   Is That a Hen?

Structures	Vocabulary		Phonics
• Is this a hen? / Is that a hen?	cow	cat	Short Vowel i
Yes, it is. / No, it isn't. It's a duck.	hen	dog	
• What's this? It's a cow.	horse	duck	
• What's that? It's a dog.	rabbit	this	
	pig	that	

Unit 4   This Is My Brother, Ken

Structures	Vocabulary		Phonics
• This is my brother, Ken.	grandfather	brother	Short Vowel o
• That is my cat, Max.	grandmother	sister	
• This is Fred.	father	family	
• Nice to meet you.	mother	friend	
Nice to meet you, too.			

Review 2

Unit 5 I Like Bread

Structures	Vocabulary		Phonics
• I like bread. How about you? I like bread, too. • I like chicken and salad. • Is this soup? Yes, it is. • What's this? It's popcorn.	bread soup salad pizza fish	chicken milk popcorn cake	Short Vowel u

Unit 6 How Many Apples?

Structures	Vocabulary		Phonics
• How many apples? Four apples. • Three kiwis and six apples. • I like bananas.	watermelons apples bananas pears	oranges kiwis lemons one ~ ten	Short Vowel e
Review 3			

Unit 7 What Color Is It?

Structures	Vocabulary		Phonics
• What color is it? It's orange. • I like orange. • I like green and black. • I'm sorry. That's okay.	pink orange green black white purple	brown gray red blue yellow	Review: Short Vowels

Unit 8 Close the Door, Please

Structures	Vocabulary		Phonics
• Sit down, please. Okay. • Thank you. You're welcome.	sit down stand up come here open the door close the door	open the window close the window catch the ball open the box	Ending Letters ck, ng
Review 4			

Midterm TEST 2A

Institute

Name

Score ____ /100

1 Listen and choose.
잘 듣고 알맞은 그림을 고르세요.

ⓐ

ⓑ

ⓒ

ⓓ

2 Listen and choose.
잘 듣고 그림에 알맞은 말을 고르세요.

6

ⓐ ⓑ  ⓒ  ⓓ

[7-8] Listen and choose.
잘 듣고 알맞은 그림을 고르세요.

7 ⓐ  ⓑ

ⓒ 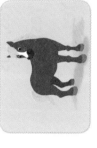 ⓓ

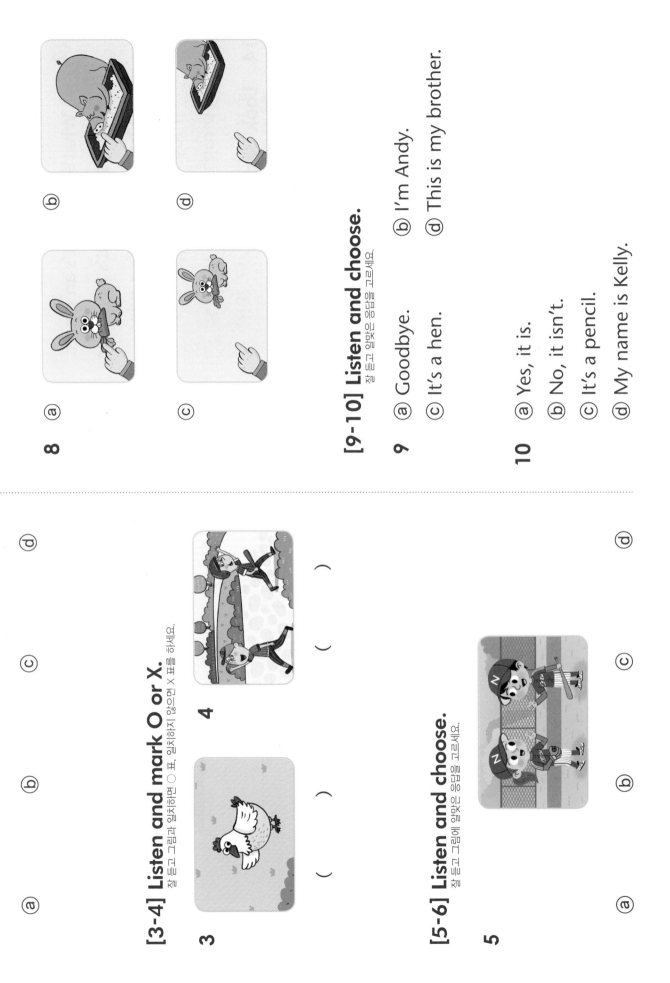

8

ⓐ ⓑ ⓒ ⓓ

[9-10] Listen and choose.
잘 듣고 알맞은 응답을 고르세요.

9
ⓐ Goodbye.　　ⓑ I'm Andy.
ⓒ It's a hen.　　ⓓ This is my brother.

10
ⓐ Yes, it is.
ⓑ No, it isn't.
ⓒ It's a pencil.
ⓓ My name is Kelly.

[3-4] Listen and mark O or X.
잘 듣고 그림과 일치하면 ○표, 일치하지 않으면 X표를 하세요.

3 (　)

4 (　)　(　)

ⓐ ⓑ ⓒ ⓓ

[5-6] Listen and choose.
잘 듣고 그림에 알맞은 응답을 고르세요.

5

ⓐ ⓑ ⓒ ⓓ

Final TEST 2A

Institute

Name

Score　　/100

[1-2] Listen and choose.
잘 듣고 알맞은 그림을 고르세요.

1

ⓐ

ⓑ

ⓒ

ⓓ

2

ⓐ

ⓑ

ⓒ

ⓓ

[6-7] Listen and choose.
그림에 알맞은 응답을 고르세요.

6

ⓐ　　ⓑ　　ⓒ　　ⓓ

7

ⓐ　　ⓑ　　ⓒ　　ⓓ

8 Listen and choose.
잘 듣고 알맞은 그림을 고르세요.

ⓐ

ⓑ

ⓒ

ⓓ

[9-10] Listen and choose.
잘 듣고 알맞은 응답을 고르세요.

9 ⓐ It's green.　　ⓑ I like kiwis.

ⓒ Six kiwis.　　ⓓ Seven lemons.

10 ⓐ Okay.　　ⓑ Good.

ⓒ Look!　　ⓓ Yes, it is.

---

3 Listen and choose.
잘 듣고 그림에 알맞은 말을 고르세요.

ⓐ　　ⓑ　　ⓒ　　ⓓ

[4-5] Listen and mark O or X.
잘 듣고 그림과 일치하면 ○ 표, 일치하지 않으면 X 표를 하세요.

4

(　　)

5

(　　)

Unit 1 p. 4

Unit 4 p. 30

Unit 5 p. 40

2nd Edition

LET'S GO

to the English World

2A

Word Book
& Workbook

CHUNJAE EDUCATION, INC.

Word Book

Hi, I'm Jack

A Listen and repeat. 01 02

hi
안녕 (만날 때 인사)

Hi, Amy.
안녕, 에이미.

hello
안녕 (만날 때 인사)

Hello, I'm Jane.
안녕, 나는 제인이야.

bye
잘 가, 안녕 (헤어질 때 인사)

Bye, Kevin.
안녕, 케빈.

goodbye
잘 가, 안녕 (헤어질 때 인사)

Goodbye, Ann.
잘 가, 앤.

what
무엇

What's your name?
네 이름은 무엇이니?

name
이름

My **name** is Sam.
내 이름은 샘이야.

my
나의

My name is Kate.
내 이름은 케이트야.

your
너의

What's **your** name?
네 이름은 무엇이니?

1 hi
안녕

2 hello
안녕

3 bye
잘 가, 안녕

4 goodbye
잘 가, 안녕

5 what
무엇

6 name
이름

7 my
나의

8 your
너의

Learn More

| I | 나는, 내가 | I am Jack. 나는 잭이야. |
| **I'm (= I am)** | 나는 ~이다 | I'm Jane. 나는 제인이야. |

Ⓐ Listen and repeat. 14 15

bag
가방

It's a bag.
그것은 가방이야.

ball
공

It's a ball.
그것은 공이야.

book
책

It's a book.
그것은 책이야.

pencil case
필통

It's a pencil case.
그것은 필통이야.

pencil
연필

It's a pencil.
그것은 연필이야.

ruler
자

It's a ruler.
그것은 자야.

eraser
지우개

It's an eraser.
그것은 지우개야.

notebook
공책, 노트

It's a notebook.
그것은 공책이야.

B Read, write, and say.

1 bag
가방

2 ball
공

3 book
책

4 pencil case
필통

5 pencil
연필

6 ruler
자

7 eraser
지우개

8 notebook
공책, 노트

Learn More

this	이것	This is a bag.	이것은 가방이야.
that	저것	That is a pencil.	저것은 연필이야.
what	무엇	What's this?	이것은 무엇이니?
nice	멋진	It's nice.	멋지다.

Is That a Hen?

A Listen and repeat. 27 28

cow
젖소

It's a cow.
그것은 젖소야.

hen
암탉

It's a hen.
그것은 암탉이야.

horse
말

Is this a horse?
이것은 말이니?

rabbit
토끼

Is this a rabbit?
이것은 토끼니?

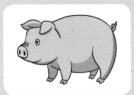

pig
돼지

Is this a pig?
이것은 돼지니?

cat
고양이

Is that a cat?
저것은 고양이니?

dog
개

Is that a dog?
저것은 개니?

duck
오리

Is that a duck?
저것은 오리니?

(B) Read, write, and say.

☐ Read ☐ Write ☐ Say

1 **cow**
젖소

2 **hen**
암탉

3 **horse**
말

4 **rabbit**
토끼

5 **pig**
돼지

6 **cat**
고양이

7 **dog**
개

8 **duck**
오리

Learn More

Look! 봐!

Yes, it is. 응, 그래.

No, it isn't. 아니, 그렇지 않아.

It's fun. 재미있어.

This Is My Brother, Ken

A Listen and repeat. 40 41

grandfather
할아버지

This is my grandfather.
이분은 나의 할아버지셔.

grandmother
할머니

This is my grandmother.
이분은 나의 할머니셔.

father
아버지

This is my father.
이분은 나의 아버지셔.

mother
어머니

This is my mother.
이분은 나의 어머니셔.

brother
남자 형제(남동생, 오빠, 형)

This is my brother, **Ken.**
이 애는 나의 남동생, 켄이야.

sister
여자 형제(여동생, 언니, 누나)

This is my sister, **Tina.**
이 애는 나의 여동생, 티나야.

family
가족

This is my family.
이것은 나의 가족이야.

friend
친구

This is my friend, **Lisa.**
이 애는 나의 친구 리사야.

☐ Read ☐ Write ☐ Say

1 grandfather
할아버지

2 grandmother
할머니

3 father
아버지

4 mother
어머니

5 brother
남자 형제

6 sister
여자 형제

7 family
가족

8 friend
친구

Learn More

this 이 사람, 이분   This **is Fred.** 이 애는 프레드야.

that 저 사람, 저분   That **is my father.** 저분은 나의 아버지셔.

Nice to meet you. 만나서 반가워.

Nice to meet you, too. 나도 만나서 반가워.

Ⓐ Listen and repeat. 53 54

bread
빵

It's bread**.**
그것은 빵이야.

soup
수프

It's soup**.**
그것은 수프야.

salad
샐러드

Is this salad**?**
이것은 샐러드니?

pizza
피자

Is this pizza**?**
이것은 피자니?

fish
생선, 물고기

I like fish**.**
나는 생선을 좋아해.

chicken
닭고기, 치킨

I like chicken**.**
나는 치킨을 좋아해.

milk
우유

I like milk**, too.**
나도 우유를 좋아해.

popcorn
팝콘

I like popcorn**, too.**
나도 팝콘을 좋아해.

Read, write, and say.

1 bread
빵

2 soup
수프

3 salad
샐러드

4 pizza
피자

5 fish
생선, 물고기

6 chicken
닭고기, 치킨

7 milk
우유

8 popcorn
팝콘

Learn More

like	좋아하다	I like milk. 나는 우유를 좋아해.
too	또한	I like milk, too. 나도 우유를 좋아해.
and	그리고	I like bread and soup. 나는 빵과 수프를 좋아해.
please	~주세요	Chicken, please. 치킨 주세요.

How about you? 너는 어때?

How Many Apples?

Ⓐ Listen and repeat. 🎧66 🎧67

watermelons 수박(여러 개)
(수박 한 개: a watermelon)

Two watermelons.
수박 2개요.

apples 사과(여러 개)
(사과 한 개: an apple)

Three apples.
사과 3개요.

bananas 바나나(여러 개)
(바나나 한 개: a banana)

Four bananas.
바나나 4개요.

pears 배(여러 개)
(배 한 개: a pear)

Five pears.
배 5개요.

oranges 오렌지(여러 개)
(오렌지 한 개: an orange)

Six oranges.
오렌지 6개요.

kiwis 키위(여러 개)
(키위 한 개: a kiwi)

Seven kiwis.
키위 7개요.

lemons 레몬(여러 개)
(레몬 한 개: a lemon)

Eight lemons.
레몬 8개요.

B Read, write, and say.

1 watermelons
수박 (여러 개)

2 apples
사과 (여러 개)

3 bananas
바나나 (여러 개)

4 pears
배 (여러 개)

5 oranges
오렌지 (여러 개)

6 kiwis
키위 (여러 개)

7 lemons
레몬 (여러 개)

Learn More

Numbers	
1 one	6 six
2 two	7 seven
3 three	8 eight
4 four	9 nine
5 five	10 ten

How many balls? 공이 몇 개니?

How about you? 너는 어때?

I like bananas. 나는 바나나를 좋아해.

UNIT 7 What Color Is It?

A Listen and repeat. 🎧79 🎧80

pink
분홍색

It's pink.
그것은 분홍색이야.

orange
주황색

It's orange.
그것은 주황색이야.

green
초록색

It's green.
그것은 초록색이야.

black
검은색

It's black.
그것은 검은색이야.

white
흰색

I like white.
나는 흰색을 좋아해.

purple
보라색

I like purple.
나는 보라색을 좋아해.

brown
갈색

I like brown.
나는 갈색을 좋아해.

gray
회색

I like gray.
나는 회색을 좋아해.

14

B Read, write, and say.

1 pink
분홍색

2 orange
주황색

3 green
초록색

4 black
검은색

5 white
흰색

6 purple
보라색

7 brown
갈색

8 gray
회색

Learn More

red 빨간색   **yellow** 노란색   **blue** 파란색

color 색깔   What color is it? 그것은 무슨 색깔이니?

and 그리고   It's green and black. 그것은 초록색과 검은색이야.

I'm sorry. 미안해.   That's okay. 괜찮아.

Close the Door, Please

sit down
앉다

Sit down, **please.**
앉으세요.

stand up
일어서다

Stand up, **please.**
일어서세요.

come here
여기로 오다

Come here, **Max.**
여기로 와, 맥스.

open the door
문을 열다

Open the door, **please.**
문을 열어 주세요.

close the door
문을 닫다

Close the door, **please.**
문을 닫아 주세요.

open the window
창문을 열다

Open the window, **please.**
창문을 열어 주세요.

close the window
창문을 닫다

Close the window, **please.**
창문을 닫아 주세요.

catch the ball
공을 잡다

Catch the ball, **Judy.**
공을 잡아, 주디.

B **Read, write, and say.**

1 **sit down**
앉다

2 **stand up**
일어서다

3 **come here**
여기로 오다

4 **open the door**
문을 열다

5 **close the door**
문을 닫다

6 **open the window**
창문을 열다

7 **close the window**
창문을 닫다

8 **catch the ball**
공을 잡다

Learn More

please ~해 주세요

Okay. 알았어. (대답하는 말)

Thank you. 고마워.

You're welcome. 천만에.

Open the box. 상자를 열어.

Workbook

Hi, I'm Jack

Words

A Check and trace.

1

☐ bye   ☐ hello

2

☐ hello   ☐ goodbye

3

☐ hi   ☐ goodbye

4

☐ hi   ☐ bye

5

☐ name   ☐ your

6

☐ my   ☐ what

7

☐ my   ☐ your

8
☐ my   ☐ your

Practice

(A) Look and match.

1

2

3

Hello, Eva.

My name is Sam.

Goodbye, Kevin.

(B) Read and choose.

1

Hello, I'm Sam.

ⓐ Hi, I'm Rita.

ⓑ Goodbye, Jack.

2

What's your name?

ⓐ Hello, Jane.

ⓑ My name is Min.

Listen & Talk

Ⓐ Read, match, and number.

1
Hi, I'm Emily.

2
Goodbye, Lily.

3
Hi, I'm Sally.
What's your name?

• My name is Kate.

• Hello, I'm Fred.

• Bye, Sam.

Ⓑ Look and write.

Goodbye   What's   I'm

1

A: Hi, I'm Emily.

_____ your name?

B: Hello, _____ Ken.

2

A: _____, Emily.

B: Bye, Ken.

22

Write & Talk

A Look and write.

1

A: _____, Kate.

B: Hi, Ben.

2

A: Bye, Tom.

B: _____, Tina.

3

A: Hello, I'm Jack.

B: Hi. My _____ is Judy.

4

A: _____ Lily.

What's your _____?

B: My name is Ann.

5

A: Hi, _____ name is Mia.

_____ your name?

B: Hello. _____ Kevin.

Story

A Look and write.

| Hello | I'm | What's | Goodbye |

1 _____, I'm Willy.

Hi!

2 _____, Willy.   Bye.

B Look and write.

1 _____, Emily.

Hello, Kevin.

2 _____ your name?

_____ _____ is Ann.

3 _____, I'm Emma.

What's _____ _____?

Hi, _____ Mike.

24

Writing

A Make the sentence.

1

| Betty | Hello, | . |

····▶ _____

안녕, 베티.

2

| Andy | Goodbye, | . |

····▶ _____

잘 가, 앤디.

3

| I'm | Hello, | Brad | . |

····▶ _____

안녕, 나는 브래드야.

4

| name | What's | ? | your |

····▶ _____

네 이름은 무엇이니?

5

| is | Rita | name | . | My |

····▶ _____

내 이름은 리타야.

What's This?

Words

Ⓐ Trace and match.

1 book

2 pencil

3 bag

4 eraser

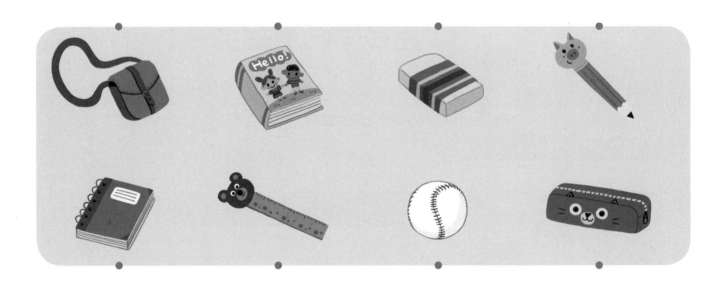

5 notebook

6 ball

7 pencil case

8 ruler

Practice

(A) Read and choose.

1 It's a ruler.

① ②

2 It's a pencil.

① ②

3 It's a notebook.

① ②

4 It's an eraser.

① ②

(B) Circle and write.

1

A: What's this?

B: It's a _____.
(ball / notebook)

2

A: What's that?

B: It's a _____.
(ruler / pencil case)

Listen & Talk

Ⓐ Circle, match, and trace.

1 What's [this? / that?]  •   • It's a ball.

2 What's [this? / that?]  •   • It's a book.

3 What's [this? / that?]  •   • It's a pencil.

Ⓑ Write and circle.

1

A: What's _____?

B: It's (a / an) _____.

2

A: What's _____?

B: It's (a / an) _____.

Write & Talk

Ⓐ Look and write.

1

A: What's _____?

B: It's a pencil case.

2

A: _____ that?

B: It's a _____.

3

A: What's _____?

B: _____ an eraser.

4

A: What's _____?

B: It's a _____.

A: It's nice.

5

A: What's _____?

B: It's a bag.

A: What's that?

B: It's a _____.

Story

A Choose and write.

| What's that? | It's a pencil. | It's a book. |

1

It's a ball.

2

B Follow and write.

1

A: What's _____?

B: It's an _____.

2

A: _____ this?

B: It's a _____.

3

A: What's _____?

B: It's a _____.

Writing

A Make the sentence.

1

| this | ? | What's |

····▶ _____

이것은 무엇이니?

2

| ? | that | What's |

····▶ _____

저것은 무엇이니?

3

| a | . | It's | pencil case |

····▶ _____

그것은 필통이야.

4

| eraser | is | an | . | This |

····▶ _____

이것은 지우개야.

5

| is | That | . | notebook | a |

····▶ _____

저것은 공책이야.

Is That a Hen?

Words

A Match and write.

1

_____

2

_____

3

_____

4

_____

pig

hen

horse

cow

dog

cat

rabbit

duck

5

_____

6

_____

7

_____

8

_____

Practice

A Read and check.

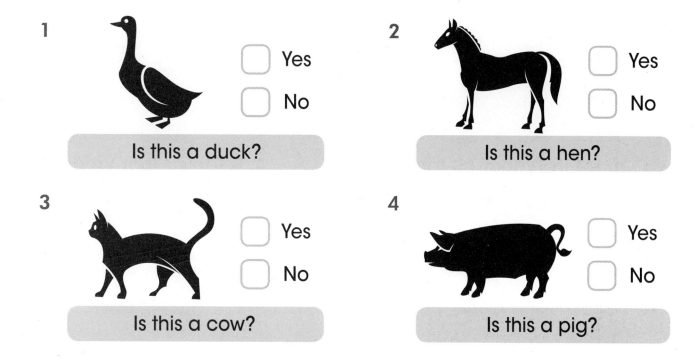

1 Is this a duck?

Yes
No

2 Is this a hen?

Yes
No

3 Is this a cow?

Yes
No

4 Is this a pig?

Yes
No

B Read and circle.

1

A: Is this a rabbit?

B: (Yes, it is. / No, it isn't.)

2

A: Is this a pig?

B: (Yes, it is. / No, it isn't.)

3

A: Is this a cow?

B: (Yes, it is. / No, it isn't.)

Listen & Talk

(A) Look and circle.

1

A: Is (this / that) a rabbit?

B: (Yes, it is. / No, it isn't.)

2

A: Is (this / that) a dog?

B: (Yes, it is. / No, it isn't.)

3

A: Is (this / that) a cat?

B: (Yes, it is. / No, it isn't.)

4

A: Is (this / that) a hen?

B: (Yes, it is. / No, it isn't.)

(B) Look and write.

| that | this | Yes | No |

1

A: Is _____ a cow?

B: _____, it isn't. It's a horse.

2

A: Is _____ a duck?

B: _____, it is.

Write & Talk

A Look and write.

1

A: Is that a _____ ?

B: Yes, _____ is.

2

A: _____ this a duck?

B: No, it isn't. It's a _____ .

3

A: Is this a dog?

B: _____ , it isn't. It's a _____ .

4

A: What's that?

Is that a _____ ?

B: Yes, it _____ .

5

A: What's this?

Is this a hen?

B: No, it _____ . It's a _____ .

Story

Ⓐ Look and number.

1

ⓐ
ⓑ

| | Yes, it is. |

| | Is this a pig? |

2

ⓒ
ⓓ

| | Is that a horse? |

| | No, it isn't. It's a cat. |

Ⓑ Look and write.

1   2   3

1   A: Is that a cow?

   B: _____, _____ _____. It's a _____.

2   A: Look! _____ that a _____?

   B: Yes, it is.

3   A: Is _____ a duck?

   B: _____, _____ _____. It's a _____.

Writing

Ⓐ Make the sentence.

1

| that | Is | a cat | ? |

····▶ _____

저것은 고양이니?

2

| ? | Is | a pig | this |

····▶ _____

이것은 돼지니?

3

| a horse | Is | ? | that |

····▶ _____

저것은 말이니?

4

| Is | a dog | ? | this |

····▶ _____

이것은 개니?

5

| a duck | ? | that | Is |

····▶ _____

저것은 오리니?

This Is My Brother, Ken

Words

(A) Look and write.

mother	father	sister
brother	grandmother	grandfather

1

2

3

This is
my family

me

4

5

6

Practice

A Read and choose.

1  This is my grandmother.

     ⓐ    ⓑ

2  This is my father.

     ⓐ    ⓑ

3  This is my sister.

     ⓐ    ⓑ

B Check and write.

This is my _____, Ken.

☐ sister   ☐ brother

I'm Tina. Nice to meet you, Ken.

_____, too.

☐ This is my sister

☐ Nice to meet you

Listen & Talk

A Circle and write.

1

father

mother

2

mother

father

3

grandfather

grandmother

4

sister

brother

1 This is _____ _____.

2 _____ is my _____.

3 This _____ my _____.

4 This is _____ _____.

B Look and check.

1

This is my grandfather. ☐

This is my grandmother. ☐

Hello, I'm Fred.

Nice to meet you, Fred.

2

This is my friend, Kate. ☐

Nice to meet you, Amy. ☐

Nice to meet you, too.

Write & Talk

(A) Look and write.

1

A: _____

B: Nice to meet you, too.

2

A: _____

B: Nice to meet you.

C: Nice to meet you, too.

3

A: _____

B: Hello, I'm Kevin.

Nice to meet you.

A: Nice to meet you, too.

4

A: Julie, this my grandmother.

B: Nice to meet you, Julie.

C: _____

Hi, my name is Tim.	This is my brother.
Nice to meet you, too.	Nice to meet you.

Story

A Read and number in the order.

1

☐ This is my father.

☐ Nice to meet you, too.

☐ Hello, I'm Fred. Nice to meet you.

2

☐ Hi, Fred. Nice to meet you.

☐ Nice to meet you, too.

☐ Mom, this is Fred.

B Match and write.

1

A: Hello, _____ Tom.
   Nice to meet you.
B: Hi, I'm Ann.

   _____, too.

2

A: _____ Eric.
B: Hi, I'm Sue.

   _____, Eric.
C: Nice to meet you, too.

42

Writing

Ⓐ Make the sentence.

1

| father | is | my | This | . |

····▶ _____

이분은 나의 아버지셔.

2

| is | sister | . | This | my |

····▶ _____

이 사람은 나의 누나야.

3

| my | This | family | is | . |

····▶ _____

이건 나의 가족이야.

4

| meet | Nice | to | you | . |

····▶ _____

만나서 반가워.

5

| too | you, | to | Nice | . | meet |

····▶ _____

나도 만나서 반가워.

I Like Bread

Words

A Complete the puzzle.

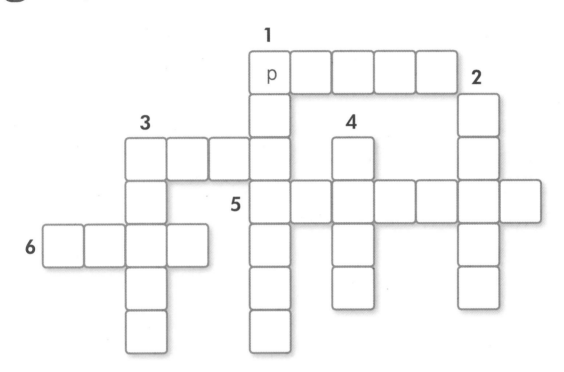

→ Across

1

3

5

6

↓ Down

1

2

3

4

soup

pizza

fish

chicken

salad

milk

popcorn

bread

Practice

(A) Read and write the letter.

1 I like milk. ☐

2 I like salad. ☐

3 I like pizza. ☐

4 I like popcorn. ☐

ⓐ

ⓑ

ⓒ

ⓓ

(B) Look and write.

| soup | fish | chicken | bread |

1

A: I like _____.

B: I like _____, too.

2

A: I like _____.

How about you?

B: I like _____, too.

Listen & Talk

(A) Circle, follow, and write.

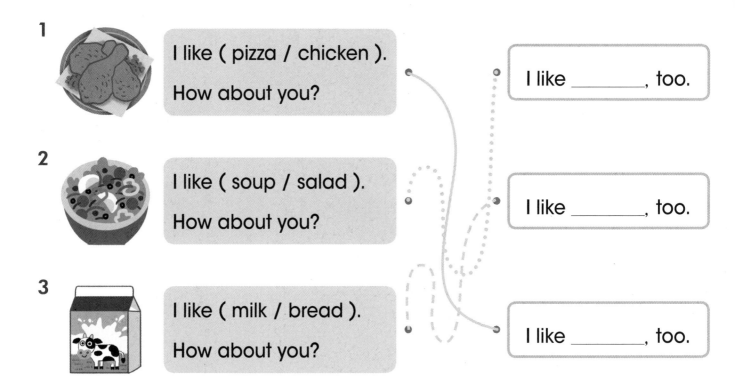

1. I like (pizza / chicken). How about you?

   I like _____, too.

2. I like (soup / salad). How about you?

   I like _____, too.

3. I like (milk / bread). How about you?

   I like _____, too.

(B) Look and write.

| you | soup | like | pizza | How |

1.
A: I like bread.

   _____ about _____?

B: I like _____.

2.
A: What's that?

B: It's _____. I _____ pizza.

46

Write & Talk

A Look and write.

1

A: I _____ chicken.

B: I like chicken, _____.

2

A: I like _____. How about you?

B: _____ _____ fish, too.

3

A: I like bread. _____ _____ _____?

B: I like pizza and _____.

4

A: What's this?

B: It's _____.

A: Oh, I _____ soup.

5

A: Is this _____?

B: Yes, it is.

A: Wow! I like _____.

Story

A Look and write.

| I like fish. | I like bread and fish. | How about you? |

1

I like bread.
_____

2

B Look and write.

😀	1	2	3	4
Ben				
Tina				

1 Ben: I like _____.

   Tina: I _____ fish, too.

2 Ben: I like _____.

   Tina: I like _____.

3 Ben: I _____ popcorn.

   How about you?

   Tina: I like _____, too.

4 Ben: I like _____.

   _____ about you?

   Tina: I like _____.

48

Writing

Ⓐ Make the sentence.

1

| fish | I | like | . |

····▶ _____

나는 생선을 좋아해.

2

| . | popcorn, | I | like | too |

····▶ _____

나도 팝콘을 좋아해.

3

| this | Is | salad | ? |

····▶ _____

이거 샐러드예요?

4

| milk. | like | I | bread | and |

····▶ _____

나는 빵과 우유를 좋아해.

5

| chicken | and | I | like | salad. |

····▶ _____

나는 치킨과 샐러드를 좋아해.

How many apples?

Words

A Look and write.

1

_____

2

_____

3

_____

4

_____

oranges

pears

apples

lemons

bananas

kiwis

watermelons

5

_____

6

_____

7

_____

Practice

(A) Match and write.

1  • • three • • lemons _____

2  • • five • • apples _____

3  • • eight • • pears *five pears*

4  • • four • • bananas _____

(B) Circle and write the letter.

ⓐ    ⓑ    ⓒ 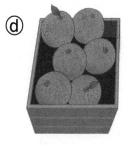   ⓓ

1
A: How many kiwis?
B: (Nine / Ten) kiwis. ◯

2
A: How many oranges?
B: (Five / Six) oranges. ◯

3
A: How many pears?
B: (Ten / Seven) pears. ◯

4
A: How many watermelons?
B: (Two / Six) watermelons. ◯

Listen & Talk

A Match and write.

1 How many bananas? •   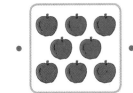   • Five _____.

2 How many pears? •      • Eight _____.

3 How many apples? •      • Six _____.

4 How many kiwis? •      • Three _____.

B Write and check.

1 A: How many _____?

   B: ⓐ Three watermelons. ☐

      ⓑ One watermelon. ☐

2 A: _____ _____ lemons?

   B: ⓐ Eight lemons. ☐

      ⓑ Seven lemons. ☐

Write & Talk

Ⓐ Look and write.

1

A: How _____ lemons?

B: Three _____.

2

A: How many _____?

B: _____ bananas.

A: Good!

3

A: _____ _____ oranges?

B: Ten _____. I like oranges.

4

A: How many _____?

B: _____ kiwis. I like kiwis.

A: I like _____, too.

5

A: _____ _____ watermelons?

B: _____ watermelon.

A: How many apples?

B: Four _____.

Story

Ⓐ Read and mark O or X.

1

Seven pears.

2

Nine bananas.

3

Five apples and
four pears.

Ⓑ Count and write.

1 A: How many _____?

  B: _____ lemons.

2 A: _____ _____ oranges?

  B: _____ oranges.

3 A: _____ _____ pears?

  B: _____ pears.

4 A: How many _____?

  B: _____ bananas.

Writing

Ⓐ Make the sentence.

1

| many | How | bananas | ? |

····▶ _____

바나나 몇 개요?

2

| ? | pears | many | How |

····▶ _____

배가 몇 개예요?

3

| lemons | . | Five |

····▶ _____

레몬 다섯 개요.

4

| Three | and | pears | two | . | apples |

····▶ _____

사과 세 개랑 배 두 개야.

5

| . | I | watermelons | like |

····▶ _____

나는 수박을 좋아해.

What Color Is It?

Words

A Trace, find, and match.

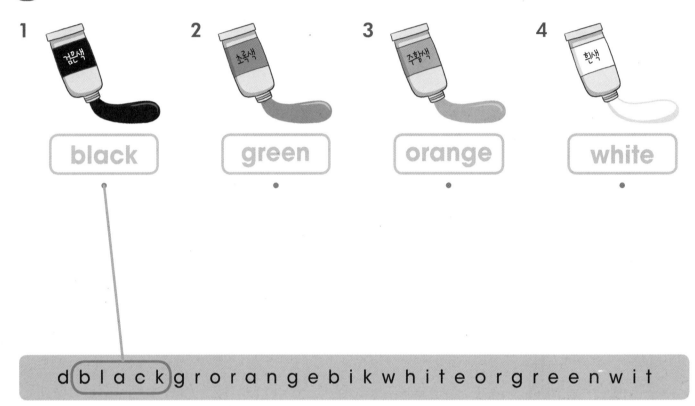

1 black

2 green

3 orange

4 white

d b l a c k g r o r a n g e b i k w h i t e o r g r e e n w i t

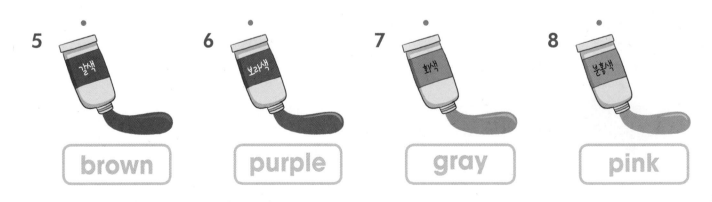

p r a p u r p l e e g r a y d r o n b r o w n p u r p i n k b h

5 brown

6 purple

7 gray

8 pink

Practice

Ⓐ Look and check.

1

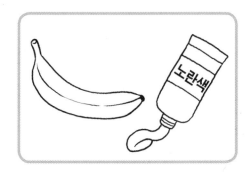

ⓐ It's black. ☐
ⓑ It's yellow. ☐

2

ⓐ It's orange. ☐
ⓑ It's purple. ☐

3

ⓐ It's white. ☐
ⓑ It's brown. ☐

4

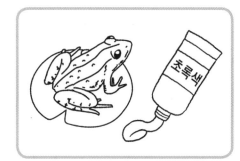

ⓐ It's gray. ☐
ⓑ It's green. ☐

Ⓑ Unscramble and write.

1

l a b c k

A: What color is it?

B: It's _____.

2

b w r n o

A: What color is it?

B: _____ _____.

3

i k n p

A: What color is it?

B: _____ _____.

Listen & Talk

(A) Write, follow, and color.

1 | What color _____ _____ ? |

2 | _____ _____ is it? |

3 | _____ _____ is it? |

It's blue.

It's gray.

It's purple.

(B) Look and write.

1

brown

A: It's a rabbit.

B: What color _____ _____ ?

A: It's _____ .

2

pink

A: Look! It's a hat.

B: It's _____ .

I like _____ .

Write & Talk

Ⓐ Look and write.

1

A: _____ color is it?

B: It's _____.

2

A: What color _____ _____?

B: It's _____ and _____.

3

A: It's blue. And it's red.

　　Look! What _____ is it?

B: It's _____.

4

A: Look! It's a pencil case.

B: It's _____. I _____ brown.

A: I like brown, too.

5

A: It's _____ and _____.

　　What is it?

B: Is it a _____?

A: Yes, it is.

Story

A Look and match.

1  보라색

2  갈색

3  초록색

I like purple.

It's green.

I like brown.

B Read and number. Then color.

1 It's a pig.

What color is it?

It's pink.

2 It's a horse.

What color is it?

It's gray.

3 It's a dog.

What color is it?

It's black.

Writing

A Make the sentence.

1

| is | color | it | What | ? |

...▶ _____

무슨 색이지?

2

| purple | . | It's |

...▶ _____

그것은 보라색이야.

3

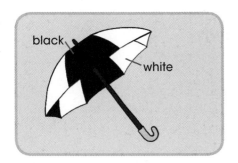

| . | like | orange | I |

...▶ _____

나는 주황색을 좋아해.

4

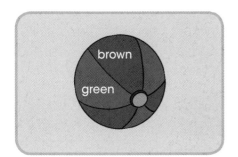

| white | It's | black | . | and |

...▶ _____

그것은 검은색과 흰색이야.

5

| brown | green | . | and | It's |

...▶ _____

그것은 초록색과 갈색이야.

Close the Door, Please

Words

Ⓐ Match and write.

1
stand •

• the window _____

2
open •

• the door _____

3
come •

• here _____

4
close •

• down _____

5
catch •

• up _____ stand up _____

6
sit •

• the ball _____

Practice

Ⓐ Look and circle.

1

(Open / Close) the door.

2

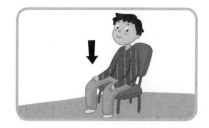

(Sit / Stand) down.

3

(Open / Close) the window.

4

(Sit / Stand) up.

Ⓑ Connect and write.

1

Sit · Stand · · up, · down, · please.

┄┄▸ _____

2

Open · Close · · the window, · the door, · please.

┄┄▸ _____

3

Come · Catch · · the ball, · here, · please.

┄┄▸ _____

Listen & Talk

Ⓐ Read and circle ○ or ✕.

1

○

✕

A: Close the window.

B: Okay.

2

○

✕

A: Stand up.

B: Okay.

3

○

✕

A: Open the door, please.

B: Okay.

4

○

✕

A: Come here, please.

B: Okay.

Ⓑ Look and write.

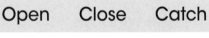

| Open | Close | Catch | ⌣ | ball | door | window |

1

A: _____ the _____, Joy.

B: Okay.

2

A: _____ the _____, Ken.

B: Okay.

Write & Talk

(A) Look and write.

1

A: _____ _____, Billy.

B: Okay.

2

A: _____ the ball, Alex!

B: _____

A: Good!

3

A: Sit _____, _____.

B: Okay. I'm sorry.

4

A: _____ the door, please.

B: _____

A: Thank you, Eric.

5

A: _____ the _____, please.

B: Okay, Dad.

A: Thank you, Emily.

Story

A Follow and write.

1

2

3

_____, please.

_____, please.

_____, Jack.

B Look and write.

A: _____ the door, _____.

B: Okay. I'm sorry.

A: Stand _____, please.

B: Okay. Sorry.

A: _____ the box, Roy.

B: Okay. Wow! It's a robot.

Thank you, Mom.

Writing

Ⓐ Make the sentence.

1

| down, | Sit | please | . |

····▶ _____

앉으세요.

2

| Joy | . | the ball, | Catch |

····▶ _____

공을 잡아, 조이.

3

| please | . | the door, | Close |

····▶ _____

문을 닫아 줘.

4

| . | here, | please | Come |

····▶ _____

여기로 와 줘.

5

| the window, | Open | please | . |

····▶ _____

창문을 열어 줘.

2nd Edition

LET'S GO
to the English World

2A